Searchlights an

by Jenny Hy
Illustrated by Simon Smith

Hello there!

I'm Jenny and I'm glad you've joined us for this **Livewires** adventure. I wonder if you like secrets, because in this adventure the Livewires discover all kinds of rather special secrets or puzzles which help them to find out more about Jesus. On some pages they need your help as well—oh, and don't forget to take a break with the Livewires on the diary pages. You can even write in the things that you're doing if you want to—just put the date on the right day to remind you.

So let's go and join the Livewires in Annie-log's bedroom. I'll leave Little Ben to introduce you to everyone...

Text copyright © Jenny Hyson 1997

Illustrations copyright © Simon Smith 1997

The author asserts the moral right to be identified as the author of this work.

Published by
The Bible Reading Fellowship
Peter's Way, Sandy Lane West
Oxford OX4 5HG
ISBN 0 7459 3550 8

First edition 1997

10 9 8 7 6 5 4 3 2 1 0

All rights reserved

Acknowledgments
Unless otherwise stated, scripture quotations are taken from the Good News Bible published by The Bible Societies/HarperCollins Publishers Ltd UK © American Bible Society, 1966, 1971, 1976, 1992.

A catalogue record for this book is available from the British Library.

Printed and bound in Malta by Interprint Limited

An imprint of
The Bible Reading Fellowship

Hi there!

If you've not met us before let me introduce you to my friends. Tim's the one on the floor with Tempo—Tempo's Tim's dog—he's the one with four legs! On the top bunk, reading a book, is Quartz. She loves dancing (unlike her twin brother, Digit, who's much more interested in drawing brilliant pictures in his sketchbook). If you're lucky you may get to see one of his cartoons.

Annie-log is sitting at Boot. He's an amazing computer who whisks us away to all kinds of places when words or Bible verses are typed onto his keyboard. He lands us in all kinds of situations, and then follows us on his special rollerblades, with Tychi his mouse as large as life and twice as clever! Annie-log has a younger sister called Data—that's her lying on the floor reading a comic. And you've probably guessed that I'm the one on the bottom bunk! We all like to get together, especially at the weekends when there's no school, and that's how this particular adventure began...

It was the weekend and the Livewires were just wondering what to do when Tim suggested playing a game of hide and seek. There weren't many places to hide in Annie-log's bedroom so they decided to go out into the garden instead. Tempo got really excited when he heard the word garden—he liked to explore and dig holes. Annie-log was sitting at the computer, so she typed the word 'garden' on Boot's keyboard. There was a whooshing noise and the next minute they found themselves in a garden, but it wasn't Annie-log's...

The Livewires were about to run off and hide when Tempo started barking again. They went to find out where he was...

Copy the apple shape onto a piece of paper and cut out six apples altogether. Punch a small hole in the top of each apple. Unscramble the letters to find out what garden you think the children have landed in. Write your answer on one of the apple shapes.

het drenga fo dnee

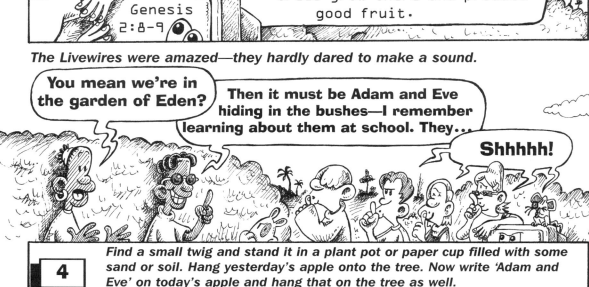

DIARY

SUNDAY
The Bible said that the tree in the garden was growing fruit. People often think of the fruit as being apples. What fruit do you think the tree was growing?

MONDAY
What other kinds of trees do you think God planted in the garden?

TUESDAY
Do you ever try and hide when you've done something wrong? Sometimes we hide behind a lie when we've done something wrong.

WEDNESDAY
Do you think it is right to be punished when you've done something wrong? Why?

THURSDAY
What kind of things do you find it hard to say 'No' to?

FRIDAY
Have you ever planted vegetables in a garden or an allotment? What kinds of things did you grow?

SATURDAY
On the last apple shape write a short prayer thanking God for all the fruit and vegetables that grow in our world.

Boot had landed the Livewires on a mountain. It was dark and Little Ben was scared.

"H... h... h... has anyone g... g... got a torch?"

Digit fished in his pocket, bringing out all kinds of bits and pieces. Finally he found a small torch, and switched it on.

"There you are, Little Ben. It's not much of a light, but it's better than nothing."

Little Ben took the torch and flashed it around. They realized it was misty, like being in the clouds. Through the mist they could just make out the shadow of someone standing nearby.

"Who's that?"

"I don't know. I don't think he's seen us. He seems to be listening to something."

"Listen! Can you hear it?"

"Hear what?"

"It's that voice again."

"What voice?"

"The one we heard in the garden."

Everyone stopped to listen.

"Yes, there it is again—I can't hear it very well because of the wind..."

The Livewires strained their ears to catch the sound of the voice in the wind.

"I m the L rd y ur G d wh br ught y u ut f Egypt where y u were sl ves. W rship n ther g d but me... Respect y ur F ther nd y ur M ther..."

The wind is blowing so hard that all the 'o's and 'a's have been blown away. Can you fill in the missing words lost in the wind?

Wow! Is God still speaking to Adam and Eve, Boot?

10

Boot gave an impatient bleep.

Exodus 24:12

The Lord said to Moses, "Come up the mountain to me, and while you are here, I will give you two stone tablets which contain all the laws that I have written for the instruction of the people."

The Livewires watched from the hillside as Moses strode into the camp. He threw the two tablets of stone to the ground and they broke into pieces. Quartz came running back up the hill.

"Did you see that? Moses is really angry. He's broken the tablets of stone that God wrote the commandments on."

"Yes, we saw him."

"Now he's pulling down the golden statue."

The children stood and watched as the statue tumbled over and the people began to run away.

"I wonder where the people got the gold from to build the statue in the first place?"

"There must have been a lot of earrings!"

Aaron said to them, "Take off the gold earrings which your wives, your sons, and your daughters are wearing, and bring them to me." He took the earrings, melted them, poured the gold into a mould, and made a gold bull calf.

Exodus 32: 2 & 4

"But why did they do it when they knew it was wrong?"

"Because Moses was such a long time up the mountain that the people got impatient and told Aaron to make another god who could lead them."

"Did God forgive the people for worshipping the statue?"

"I don't know. But look, there's Moses going back up the mountain. That mist is coming down again—let's go and shelter under that tree."

Put the broken pieces of the stone tablets back together to find out another of the commandments. Now write it with the others on your cards.

Keep the Sabbath holy

13

The Ark of the Covenant was very important to the Israelites and they took great care of it. Can you work out how big the box was from the measurements Boot has given? The box was covered in pure gold, so it must have been very heavy.

Sometimes we can see something someone else has and wish that we could have it. God says that we must not envy another person's possessions.

Add this commandment to the others.

DIARY

SUNDAY
The Livewires had to listen hard to hear what God was saying to Moses. When you pray don't forget to listen to what God has to say to you.

MONDAY
Is there a commandment that you know which isn't on the list? If there is, add it to the list. If you can't think of one, you might like to add something that you think would make a good commandment.

TUESDAY
Is there something that is important to you? What is it?

WEDNESDAY
Do you sometimes get impatient and then do something wrong? Ask God to help you to be more patient.

THURSDAY
Look at your list of commandments—have you got ten? You might like to look up Exodus 20:1–17 and fill in the ones that are missing. (Exodus is the second book in the Bible.)

FRIDAY
Think of something you could do to help you remember God's commandments.

SATURDAY
Psalm 119 is a song all about the commandments. As you colour in the verse below, remember that God wants us to obey the commandments, not because he wants to control us, but because he loves us and knows what's best for us.

Lord you have given us your Laws and told us to obey them faithfully
How I hope I shall be faithful
In keeping your instructions

Psalm 119: 4–5

The Livewires rolled down and down and found themselves at the bottom of the hill. They landed in a tangle of arms and legs amongst a crowd of people. Several people turned to them and said, 'Shhh'.

The Livewires untangled themselves and sat down to listen. Tim was holding Tempo's lead. Tempo had smelt something interesting in one of the people's bags.

Tempo's lead is tangled round the Livewires legs!
Can you see which lead belongs to Tempo and help to unravel it?

"Happy are those who are merciful to others; God will be merciful to them!"

Matthew 5:7

What does merciful mean?

It's like forgiving someone and not paying them back even when they've done something wrong.

Like when I broke Digit's headphones—he was really upset but he didn't go and break mine.

God was merciful to the Israelites when they worshipped the statue, wasn't he?

Yes, that's right—it's not always easy to forgive.

The Livewires sat and thought about this. Tempo wandered off, sniffing round another group of people.

Tempo, come here. I think he's hungry, aren't you boy?

Tempo came back to Tim, wagging his tail, and tried to lick him. Digit dug deep into his pocket and pulled out a dog biscuit.

Mercy is not a word we use very much today, but we might talk about 'getting our own back' or 'getting revenge', which is the opposite of mercy. Can you think of times when you have wanted to 'get your own back' on someone who has upset you? Jesus said 'Happy are those who are merciful to others.'

Which of these things do you think show mercy?

Forgiving someone even though they got you into trouble.

Helping someone who is hurt even though they often make fun of you.

Refusing to share crayons because the other person never shares.

18

"Happy are those who are humble; they will receive what God has promised!"

Little Ben started to lose interest and played with Digit's torch, flashing the light on and off. Digit tried to snatch the torch back off Little Ben. An argument broke out.

Stop wasting the battery!

I'm not, I'm looking for worms.

Little Ben started to shine the torch into the grass.

Give the torch back to me!

No, I'm using it.

Little Ben and Digit started to fight.

"Happy are those who work for peace; God will call them his children!"

Matthew 5:9

Annie-log pulled Digit and Little Ben apart.

Come on, you two, stop fighting. Jesus says we should work for peace, not fight and get angry with one another.

Little Ben and Digit said sorry to each other and sat down. Little Ben put the torch back in his pocket.

The dove is often seen as a sign of peace. Copy the picture of the dove, cut it out and hang it up somewhere to remind you that Jesus tells us to work for peace. If you've got some white feathers you might like to stick them onto your dove.

See if you can find five daisy chains, four worms and two bars of chocolate on this page.

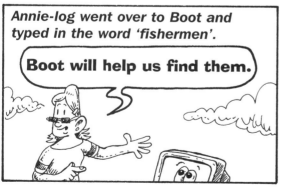

How many words can you make from the word 'fishermen'?
There are at least 15.

fishermen

fish, her, men, is, she, rim, hen, he, see, fee, his, hem, me, fin, mine...

DIARY

SUNDAY
Have you got a favourite Bible story? Which one is it and why do you like it?

MONDAY
Another word for mercy is compassion or sympathy. How can you show sympathy to people who are in need?

TUESDAY
Do you know which countries are at war at the moment? Look in the newspaper or on the television and make a list. Pray for peace in each of the countries and the people who live there.

WEDNESDAY
What kinds of things do you worry about? Talking to others about our worries can sometimes help and so can talking to Jesus. Why not talk to someone today if something is worrying you?

THURSDAY
Jesus' teaching that starts 'Happy are those…' is sometimes called the Beatitudes. Look in Matthew chapter 5 verses 3–11 and see how many times Jesus starts with the words 'Happy are those'. In some Bibles it might say 'Blessed are those'. ('Matthew' is the first book in the New Testament part of your Bible.)

FRIDAY
Dear Jesus, please help me to follow you always by being loving and kind to those I meet. Amen

SATURDAY
The Beatitudes are part of the 'Sermon on the Mount'. Jesus is thought to have taught them on a hill near Capernaum overlooking the sea of Galilee. Can you find it on the map?

The Livewires felt themselves moving up and down in the darkness. There was a strong smell of fish and the sound of waves.

24 *Little Ben tried the torch and this time it worked. They could see that they were in the bottom a boat full of fish! Tempo was trying to catch a fish which was flapping about in the corner of the boat.*

Luke 5:3

How many fish can you count in the boat?

In the darkness the Livewires didn't notice the fishermen at the boat's helm. Suddenly the boat jolted and the Livewires fell in a heap amongst the fish. The fishermen had jumped out of the boat and were pulling the boat up onto the beach.

What was that?

The Livewires untangled themselves and looked over the side of the boat. Through the darkness they could see that the fishermen were pulling the boat up onto the beach in the early morning light.

The children jumped out of the boat. Little Ben landed up to his ankles in the water!

I smell of fish.

So do I.

My feet are wet!

Come on! That must be Simon. He was one of Jesus' disciples. Let's go and ask him if he knew Jesus was God's son.

Dawn was just beginning to break as the Livewires went over to the fishermen and introduced themselves. Simon told the Livewires about the day they met Jesus...

```
Jesus got into one of the boats - it belonged to Simon -
and asked him to push off a little from the shore. He said
to Simon, "Push the boat out further to the deep water, and
you and your partners let down your nets for a catch."
```

Yes, we caught such a large number of fish that the nets were about to break!

Did you catch anything?

```
Jesus said to Simon, "Don't
be afraid; from now on you
         will be
           catching
             people."
```

Luke 5:3-4 & 10

25

Your funny friend is right! We just left everything—our boats, our fishing nets, everything... and followed Jesus.

Cut out five fish shapes (you'll need one for each day of this week). On today's fish, copy the words of this promise Jesus made to his disciples:

DIARY

SUNDAY
Jesus told Simon Peter that he would make him a fisher of people. What do you think he meant?

MONDAY
Write a list of all the things you could do to show that you are following Jesus.

TUESDAY
Find a piece of net (like oranges sometimes come in) or draw a large fishing net on a piece of paper. Fasten the four fish with a promise of Jesus written on them to the net.

WEDNESDAY
What do you think each of Jesus' promises means?

THURSDAY
Whose voice do you think the Livewires heard on the mountain? How does God talk to us today?

FRIDAY

> Dear Lord Jesus, help us to listen to the stories about you and learn from them how much God loves and cares for us. Amen.

SATURDAY
After Jesus was crucified the early Christians used the sign of the fish as a secret code to each other. The word fish in Greek is IXOYS and the letters stand for 'Jesus Christ God's Son Saviour'

Write this on your final fish and pin it to the fishing net.

"Jesus told stories with secrets inside them."

"What kind of stories, Tychi?"

Tychi flashed through some menus on Boot's screen and there was a loud whoosh as the Livewires were whisked into Boot's disk drive...

The Livewires had landed in a farmer's field. Almost at once the ground began to shake and shoots began to push their way through the soil right under where the Livewires had fallen.

Little Ben found himself lifted up into the air.

Ooooh!

Digit was surrounded by thorns and prickles.

Ow ow!

Tempo was barking at some big black birds.

Where are we, Boot? What's happening?

"Once there was a man who went out to sow corn. As he scattered the seed in the field, some of it fell along the path, where it was stepped on, and the birds ate it up. Some of it fell on rocky ground, and when the plants sprouted, they dried up because the soil had no moisture."

Luke 8: 5-8

Digit climbed out of the prickles.

Some seeds have fallen amongst these prickles, but they'll never grow here. They'll get choked by the thistles.

Data helped Little Ben out of the seed.

Well, these seeds are growing well. Look at how tall this one has grown!

It's all very strange. I wonder what the parable means?

Plant half a packet of cress seeds in a pot of soil and half in an egg box with wet cotton wool. See how quickly your seeds grow.

Annie-log typed 'parable?' onto Boot's keyboard, but there seemed to be a problem.

Can you solve the message of the parable?

> emoS elpoep raeh s'doG egassem tub natas slaets eht egassem yawa.
> emoS elpoep yldalg raeh s'doG egassem tub ti t'nseod knis ni. daetsnI ti steg tpews yawa dna tsol.
> emoS elpoep raeh s'doG egassem tub eht seirrow fo efil ekohc ti dna pots ti gniworg.
> emoS elpoep raeh s'doG egassem dna ti sworg dna secudorp stol fo tiurf.

"I wonder what the secret message is in this story?"

"I think the seeds are God's way of telling us how he wants us to live, being loving and caring towards each other. Some people listen to God's message and follow it, some people ignore it."

"Those people who listen to God and do what he says are like the good seed that grows really strong—like the seed that lifted Little Ben off the ground."

"This is fun."

"Do you remember any more parables?"

"There was one about a servant who wouldn't forgive, but I can't quite remember it."

"Don't worry, let's see if Boot can help us—this time without getting scrambled!"

Annie-log typed 'unforgiving servant' onto Boot. Nothing seemed to happen, so she tried again.

Boot's screen flashed and spluttered and everything went black. There was a whirring sound and then a bang. The Livewires could hear angry voices, but they couldn't see anything.

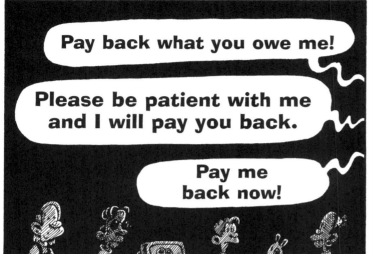

There was another flash from Boot's screen and the children found themselves in daylight again. The Livewires looked around and found they were on their own.

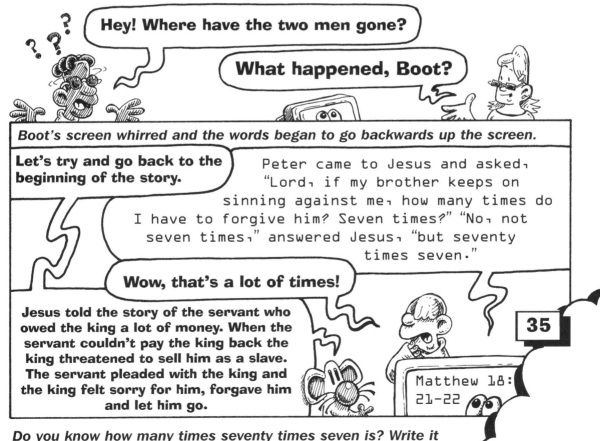

Do you know how many times seventy times seven is? Write it in the prayer cloud.

SUNDAY
Have you ever lost something that was special to you? How did you feel?

MONDAY
God thinks you are very special and he wants us to stay close to him. One of the ways we can do that is by making time to talk to him every day.

TUESDAY
Copy the sheep outline and cut it out. Colour it in and put a safety pin on the back. Wear your sheep badge to remind you that you are special to God and that he watches over you.

WEDNESDAY
When the parable talked about us producing fruit, what do you think it meant? Look up Galatians 5:22–23 in your Bible to see if you are right.

THURSDAY
In the Lord's Prayer which starts 'Our Father in heaven…' we say, 'Forgive us our sins as we forgive those who sin against us'.

Copy the words onto a piece of card and decorate it to remind you how important it is to forgive others.

FRIDAY

Dear Lord Jesus, thank you that even when I do things wrong that hurt you, I know that you will forgive me. Please help me to forgive others as completely as you forgive me. Amen.

SATURDAY
Remember to water your seeds today!

DIARY

The Livewires raced down the hill towards the well. When they arrived at the well an argument broke out as to who was first and who was last.

"I was first!"

"No you weren't, I was!"

"I would have beaten both of you, but Little Ben got in my way."

"No I didn't."

A loud bleeping sound from Boot stopped the Livewires' argument.

Jesus sat down, called the twelve disciples, and said to them, "Whoever wants to be first must place himself last of all and be the servant of all."

"That means Little Ben should get the first drink of water from the well because he arrived last."

"That's not fair! I spotted the well and I got here first, so I should have the first drink."

"Come on, Tim, don't let's quarrel—there is plenty of water for all of us to share."

Mark 9:35

With that, the Livewires pulled up the water from the well and had a drink. They sat on the grass to cool down.

Digit got out his sketchpad and drew a picture of the well to help him remember the lesson Jesus taught. You could help him finish his picture and then draw yourself sitting with the Livewires.

The Livewires sat in the sun and rested. They were tired after solving all the story puzzles. Tempo was sniffing the ground for interesting smells. Quartz lay on her back looking up at the sun.

Simon Peter, Andrew, James, Philip, Bartholomew...

What are you doing?

I'm trying to remember the names of the twelve disciples.

I wonder if they had many arguments.

Quite a few I expect—like the day they were arguing about which of them was the greatest.

Did Jesus hear them arguing?

Yes, he did.

Was he angry with them?

No, but he did surprise them. He took a child from the crowd and stood him in front of them and he said...

Tychi reached down and pressed a key on Boot's keyboard.

"Unless you change and become like children, you will never enter the Kingdom of heaven."

But I didn't think children were very important in the time of Jesus.

Matthew 18:3

No they weren't, which is why what Jesus said was even more amazing. Jesus went on to say...

"The greatest in the Kingdom of heaven is the one who humbles himself and becomes like this child."

Matthew 18:4

Digit drew a picture of himself in his sketchpad to remind himself that Jesus thought he was very special. Jesus thinks you are special too! Draw a picture of yourself on the sketchpad to remind yourself.

39

Quartz and Little Ben were having a competition to see who could stand on their hands for the longest when suddenly Quartz said...

The Livewires sat quietly and thought about what Data had said and about the lessons Jesus taught.

Think if there is someone you are feeling angry with. Jesus said, 'Do good to those who hate you'. Can you forgive that person and ask Jesus to help you think of something you can do for them? It's not easy, but ask Jesus to help you.

Digit wrote this prayer in his sketchpad. Perhaps you could draw a picture for him to go with it.

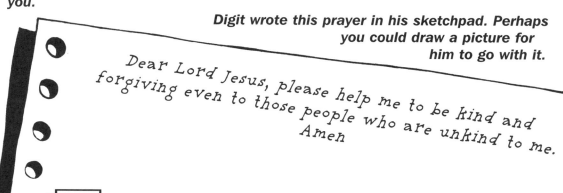

There were some very rich looking people carrying bags of money into the treasury. They seemed to be showing off as they dropped their money into the box.

Many rich men dropped in a lot of money.

Look at that elderly lady, she doesn't look like the others.

She looks very tired and poor. Who is she, Boot?

Mark 12:41

Then a poor widow came along and dropped in two little copper coins. Jesus called his disciples together and said to them, "I tell you that this poor widow put more in the offering box than all the others - she gave all she had to live on."

Mark 12: 42-44

Little Ben shone his torch around the floor when suddenly he spotted something shining in the torchlight. He bent down and found a little coin that had rolled into a crack in the floor.

I'm going to be like the poor widow and put this penny into the box.

Before the Livewires could stop him, Little Ben had joined the line of people waiting to put their money in the box. Little Ben dropped his penny into the box and then came back to where the Livewires were hiding.

Even though I only found the penny, I still wanted to give it to God.

Annie-log put her arm round Little Ben and the friends went out into the sunshine together.

Digit drew a coin in his sketchpad— what lesson do you think he wanted to remember?

As the Livewires left the temple treasury they saw a large crowd. They went to join the crowd but they couldn't see what was happening. Tim stood on his tiptoes and Little Ben tried to wriggle his way between people's legs, but it was no good. Then the Livewires saw a man walking away from the crowd looking very sad.

I wonder what is the matter. He looks very sad.

But I'm sure that's Jesus he was talking to—why should he be sad?

The man overheard the Livewires talking about him as he went past.

I've just asked Jesus what I must do to receive eternal life.

What did he say?

He told me I had to keep all the commandments.

What, like do not steal and do not commit murder?

Yes, they are the easy ones and I've kept all of those.

Then why are you so sad?

Because Jesus told me I had to sell all I had, give it to the poor and follow him. The problem is I have a really nice house and lots of clothes and servants—I can't give up all of that, it would turn my life upside down.

The man walked sadly away and the Livewires watched him go.

Jesus must have known that the things the man owned were more important to him than following Jesus. The man didn't want Jesus to turn his life upside down...

At this Boot gave a bleep. There was a whirring sound and the children found themselves on their own again, but something wasn't quite right—everything was upside down, including Boot who was standing on his head.

Jesus said to his disciples, "I assure you: it will be very hard for rich people to enter the Kingdom of heaven. It is much harder for a rich person to enter the Kingdom of God than for a camel to go through the eye of a needle."

Matthew 19:23-24

What a funny riddle—it would make a brilliant cartoon!

DIARY

SUNDAY
When did you last think something wasn't fair? What did you do? What do you think Jesus would say to you?

MONDAY
Can you help Quartz remember the names of the twelve disciples? Write down as many as you can remember and then look in your Bible at Matthew chapter 10 verses 1 and 2 to fill in the rest.

TUESDAY
Draw your own cartoon of the camel going through the eye of the needle, in the sketchpad.

WEDNESDAY
What did you draw in Digit's sketchpad to remind you that Jesus said 'Do good to those who hate you'?

THURSDAY
If you had a packet of sweets would you find it easy to share them with your friends? Even the last one?

FRIDAY
Look at your cartoon of the camel going through the eye of a needle and think if there are things you own that are maybe too important to you—are there things that you wouldn't want to share?

SATURDAY
What can you do today to show those around you that you love and care for them? Remember Jesus is talking about the people we maybe find it difficult to get along with as well.

With that Digit sat on the grass and started his drawing... upside down, of course.

Can I have my tummy tickled, please?

Hey, Boot, turn us back the right way up— the blood is rushing to our heads!

Whilst Zacchaeus and the Livewires are climbing into the sycomore tree, unscramble the letters to find the names of five more trees.

kao eecbh esohr hstctune slirev rbich ficoenr

The Livewires had climbed into the tree. Tim had pulled Data onto the branch next to him and Annie-log had lifted Little Ben onto the lowest branch. Tempo ran round the tree barking and trying to jump up to join them. Tychi pressed a key on Boot's keyboard and in a flash Boot, Tychi and Tempo were sitting in the tree with the others.

This is where it all began —from this very tree.

There is a wonderful view from up here. I can see right down the street.

I really wanted to see Jesus, and I'd run on ahead to get a good view, but because I'm only little and I wasn't very popular I soon got pushed to the back of the crowd.

Why didn't people like you?

I was the chief tax collector in the town and had to collect money from the people for the Roman Governor. I always told the people they owed more money than they actually did and then I kept the extra money for myself. That was how I became so rich. The people knew I was cheating them which was why they didn't like me, and why they pushed me out of the way when Jesus was coming.

He was trying to see who Jesus was, but he was a little man and could not see Jesus because of the crowd.

Luke 19:3

And that's why you climbed up this tree?

Yes, I could see over the top of people's heads and could see Jesus coming down the road.

Find the words in the wordsearch:

Zacchaeus, sycomore, Jesus, tax, grumbled, little, man, see, rich, tea, house, tree

47

```
L P S E E F L K O
R T Y H A D X S Y
Z A C C H A E U S
O I O I T C J S Z
R B M A N R A E T
U H O U S E E J M
M G R U M B L E D
N X E L T T I L W
```

The Livewires climbed out of the tree and followed Zacchaeus to his house. There he made them a drink and they sat on the mat to listen to the rest of the story.

It was lovely talking to Jesus, but he seemed to know all about me. I knew I was being a cheat and there and then I decided to change.

Zacchaeus stood up and said to the Lord, "Listen sir! I will give half my belongings to the poor, and if I have cheated anyone, I will pay him back four times as much."

Luke 19:8

Did you really pay everyone back?

I tried to.

Phew! That was a lot!

But lots of people seem to like you now.

That's right—it's like Jesus came and turned my life upside down.

Oh no, don't say that, I'm only just beginning to feel the right way up again!

Jesus showed Zacchaeus a better way to live that wasn't about cheating and telling lies. He helped Zacchaeus to see what he was doing wrong and helped him to change. Jesus is sad when we do things wrong, but he still loves us.

What upside down things of Jesus have we learnt about so far? Fill in the missing vowels to remind yourself.

Th- f-rst sh-ll b- l-st -nd th- l-st sh-ll b- f-rst

The gr—t-st in the k-ngd-m of h—v-n is the -ne who b-com-s like a ch-ld.

L-ve your -n-mies and do g—d to those who h-te you.

This p—r widow put m-re in the -ffering box than -ll the others.

Thank you, Lord Jesus, that even when I do something that I know is wrong you still love me and want to help me change.

The Livewires said goodbye to Zacchaeus and set off back down the road. They were glad that Jesus had helped Zacchaeus to change.

I'm glad that people like Zacchaeus now.

Yes, it must be horrible when nobody wants to talk to you because they don't trust you.

Little Ben took the torch out of his pocket and shone it at himself.

What are you doing?

I was just thinking that when Jesus talked to Zacchaeus it was like he shone a torch inside Zacchaeus, helping him to see all the things that he was doing wrong.

Boot, didn't Jesus say something about being the light of the world?

"I am the light of the world. Whoever follows me will have the light of life and will never walk in darkness."

See—like the torch shining in the darkness, helping us to see what is right.

John 8:12

When Jesus talked about darkness he was using picture language. The darkness can be the things we do wrong and make us unhappy. Jesus was saying, 'Follow me and I will be like a light showing you how to do what is right.' Which of these pictures are 'dark' pictures and which are 'light' ones? Colour the light ones in with bright colours.

50

DIARY

SUNDAY
What would fall out of your pockets if you stood upside down? Add it to the picture on page 45.

MONDAY
Have you ever wanted to see someone special and been too small to see? How did you feel? What did you do?

TUESDAY
A sycamore tree is a kind of fig tree. It would have been easier to climb than our English sycamore!

WEDNESDAY
To Jesus everyone is special—even those who, like Zacchaeus, have done something wrong.

THURSDAY
There are many poor people in our world today. Can you think of ways that you could help those who are poor and sad?

FRIDAY
Jesus turned Zacchaeus' life upside down. Is there something in your life that you would want Jesus to change? Why not ask him to help you?

SATURDAY
What are some of the ways Jesus wants us to follow him? Write them in the torch shape.

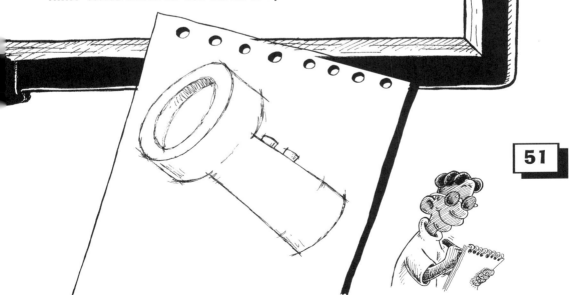

Boot's screen began to flash on and off and then everything went dark...

The Livewires stood in the darkness. The only light was from Little Ben's torch, but even that was fading.

"I think the batteries are running out. The light doesn't seem very bright."

"It feels colder."

"And what's that funny smell? It isn't fish this time!"

"I think it's incense like they burn in churches."

> The time came for Joseph and Mary to perform the ceremony of purification as the Law of Moses commanded. So they took the child to Jerusalem to present him to the Lord, as it is written in the law of the Lord: "Every firstborn male is to be dedicated to the Lord."
>
> Luke 2:22

"Did Mary and Joseph have to dedicate baby Jesus to God even though he was God's son?"

"Yes, in a way the fact that Jesus was God's son was a bit like a secret until he'd grown up. Most people who saw Jesus would have thought he was just an ordinary little boy."

Little Ben flashed his torch around.

"So where are we, and why have you brought us here, Boot?"

"There's someone Boot wants you to meet—someone who waited a long time for Jesus to come and tell the people the secrets of the kingdom of heaven. Don't you recognize where you are? You've been here before."

"But I can't see. There aren't any lights."

Annie-log typed the word 'light' into Boot, but, instead of words appearing, a beam of light shone out from the screen like a huge searchlight. Where do you think the Livewires are? Solve the riddle to find out.

52

My first is in tin and also in top.
My second is in beep but not in bop.
My third is in make and also in might.
My fourth is in pepper but not in salt.
My fifth the beginning of the word 'light'.
My sixth is in melt but not in malt.

Boot set off on his rollerblades down a series of passages. The Livewires had to run to keep up with him and the light that was shining from his screen. After a little way Boot suddenly came to a stop and the light went from his screen. The Livewires all bumped into Boot, but as they picked themselves up they noticed that the light was now coming from torches attached to pillars. Coming towards them was an elderly man with a kind face. He smiled when he saw the Livewires, and Boot introduced them.

> At that time there was a man named Simeon living in Jerusalem. He was a good, God-fearing man and was waiting for Israel to be saved.

Do you live here?

Not quite, but I do like to come into the temple whenever I can. It's a very special place—it was here I first met Jesus.

Luke 2:25

Were you here the day his mum and dad lost him?

No, I met him even before that, when he was a tiny baby not more than six weeks old.

But how did you know it was Jesus if he was still only a baby?

It's a long story! Come and sit down and I'll tell you. My old bones don't like standing for too long.

The Livewires went with Simeon and sat down to listen to what he had to say. Tempo was glad to have a chance for a sleep. He curled up and was soon dreaming about sheep! Can you help the Livewires follow Boot through the temple maze to Simeon?

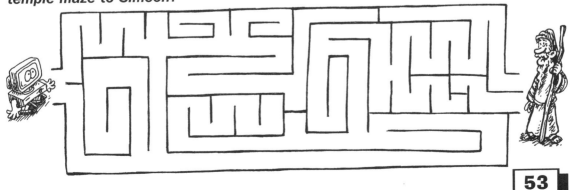

Simeon told the Livewires how he spent a lot of time in the temple because he believed that one day God would send his Messiah into the world. Simeon explained that God had promised him that he wouldn't die until he had seen the Messiah for himself.

But I thought you said that you met Jesus when he was a baby?

That's right, I did.

But how could you tell he was special—didn't he look like an ordinary baby?

He did. And yet somehow when I looked at him I knew he was God's special son— the Messiah I had been waiting for, for so many years.

What did you do?

I took the baby gently in my arms and thanked God that he'd kept his promise to me.

"Now, Lord, you have kept your promise, and you may let your servant go in peace. With my own eyes I have seen your salvation, which you have prepared in the presence of all peoples: A light to reveal your will to the Gentiles and bring glory to your people Israel."

Luke 2:29

How clever you are, Boot! Look, here comes a friend of mine. She was here in the temple that day as well.

Make a candle like the one in the diagram. In the outline of the candle write these words that Simeon spoke:

54

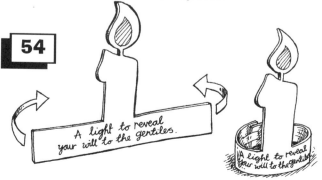

A light to reveal your will to the Gentiles.

The Livewires looked to where an elderly lady was coming towards them.

Hello, Anna, come and meet some new friends. I was just telling them about the day that young Mary and Joseph came into the temple with their new baby.

The Livewires greeted Anna and she sat down.

Did you know the baby was God's son?

Oh yes! I've seen babies brought into the temple to be dedicated to God for years—sometimes I even get to hold the babies. But I knew this baby was different. There and then I told the people in the temple that this child was from God. Of course, no one really listened, only my old friend Simeon here—but we'd been waiting for a long time to see the day when God would send the Messiah.

What did Mary and Joseph say when they heard you talk about their baby being the Messiah?

I think they were amazed, but it helped Mary to understand and believe what the angel had told her before Jesus was born.

"The angel said to her, "Don't be afraid, Mary; God has been gracious to you. You will give birth to a son, and you will name him Jesus. He will be great and will be called the Son of the Most High God."

Luke 1: 30-32

It must have been very special for Mary to have God's son.

Simeon looked at her and smiled. For a moment he was very quiet, deep in thought. Boot gave a little bleep.

"He will be a sign from God which many people will speak against and so reveal their secret thoughts."

Luke 2: 34-35

Simeon sighed and explained how he'd sadly told Mary that being Jesus' mother wouldn't be easy. She would have to go through some very sad times.

What did you mean when you said that he would be a light to reveal God's will to the Gentiles?

God has ways of showing his love to the whole world and I knew that somehow he would do just that. The prophet Isaiah wrote... Oh, what was it now? My memory isn't as good as it used to be?

"My thoughts," says the Lord, "are not like yours, and my ways are different from yours."

Isaiah 55:8

That's it! Thank you, my funny friend. God has his own way of doing what he intends, and I trusted him to show his love in his own way.

Did people think that the Messiah would be a great army leader that would fight the Romans and save them from being under their rule?

Yes, I think they did. But God sent his son to bring peace, not to make war. Jesus showed people how to love one another. That was hard for the people to understand when they were living under a foreign government.

56

Dear Lord Jesus, please help me to trust you even though I don't always understand why some things happen the way they do. Amen.

The people of Israel didn't believe Jesus was the Messiah, did they?

No, even today they are waiting for the Messiah to come and save Israel.

Tempo woke up from his sleep and started to sniff around. The Livewires heard him barking and Tim ran off to find him...

Tim found Tempo barking at some pigeons in a cage.

"Tempo, come here!"

"Tempo found some pigeons. What are they doing in the temple?"

"People have been bringing pigeons and doves or lambs to the temple since the time of Moses as a way of saying to God that they are sorry for the things they have done wrong."

The Livewires explained to Simeon and Anna how they had met Moses at the beginning of their adventures and how the people had been disobedient.

"But why do the people bring animals to say they are sorry to God? Why don't they just tell God they're sorry?"

Simeon explained that the Jewish people who worshipped in the temple still worshipped in the way that Moses had taught them. Simeon believed that the Messiah changed the way people worshipped God.

Can you find the 4 doves and 3 pigeons that Tempo frightened out of their cage?

Dear Lord Jesus, thank you that I can worship God by following you. Thank you that you are always with me. Amen

SUNDAY
Have you ever smelt incense? It has a very sweet smell. Some churches use incense when they worship God today. Can you find out why?

MONDAY
Have you ever seen a tiny baby? You might have a tiny brother or sister. What are some of the things a baby needs?

TUESDAY
Have you ever waited a long time to see someone special? How did you feel when they arrived?

WEDNESDAY
How do you think Anna felt when she saw the baby Jesus and knew he was the Messiah?

THURSDAY
Can you remember what the people had done that made Moses so angry with them?

FRIDAY
What did the Israelites do to remember God's laws?

SATURDAY
Jesus died on the cross because he loves us. Cut the shape of a cross out of a piece of card and in the centre write, 'Jesus loves me'. You could use it as a bookmark.

DIARY

The Livewires thought it was time they were going home, so they said goodbye to Anna and Simeon. Annie-log typed the word 'home' onto Boot's keyboard and pressed the return key. The children held hands, waiting for Boot to return them to Annie-log's bedroom…

There was a whirring sound from Boot and everyone felt their feet being lifted off the ground. Suddenly the whirring stopped and the Livewires noticed they were still in the temple. Annie-log pressed the return key again. They felt their feet being lifted again and when they looked around they were in a small room—but it still didn't look like Annie-log's bedroom.

I thought you were taking us home, Boot.

I think there is still something he wants to show you

The Livewires looked around. Sitting in the centre of the room around a low table was a family. They seemed to be having a meal. There were candles on the table. Annie-log opened her mouth to apologize for bursting in, but before she could say anything the lady turned and smiled at them. She invited them to come and join them at the table and the Livewires took their places. It was as if they were expected!

Wonder if this is the time to practise my begging act?

The family were talking about Jesus; how they had seen him heal people and about the wonderful stories that he told. They told the children about the dreadful day when Jesus had been crucified and how very sad they had been and then how amazed they had been when they heard how he had risen from the dead again and promised them a place in heaven.

Are you Christians?

Well, yes, but our family is also Jewish.

I didn't think that Jewish people believed Jesus was God's son.

Oh, many still don't, but those of us who have met Jesus and got to know him now realize that he is God's son—the Messiah we had all been waiting for.

```
The people
who walked in
    darkness have seen a great light.
They lived in a land of shadows,
    but now light is shining on them.
```

That's what Simeon said about Jesus!

And what Jesus said about himself.

Isaiah 9:2

John chapter 8 verse 12

Digit has written 'John chapter 8 verse 12' on his sketchpad. Can you remember what that verse says? Write it on the sketchpad.

How does Jesus make a difference to the way you worship God?

For centuries the Jewish people worshipped God in the temples, the synagogue and in their homes. Prayer, fasting, sacrifices and festivals were the basis of the Jewish religious life. Every day in their homes people were expected to pray and recite verses of scripture. Prayers were said before meals and thanks given to God for all his good gifts.

Sometimes it was very difficult—there were so many rules we had to obey, sacrifices we had to make at the temple.

We saw the pigeons and the doves in the temple—they were used for sacrifice, weren't they, to say you were sorry to God?

Yes, that's right. But after Jesus died on the cross we realized that we no longer needed to offer that kind of sacrifice. Jesus makes a difference to the way we worship God because we no longer have to make a sacrifice when we ask God's forgiveness.

But Jesus does tell us that we should forgive others.

That reminds me of a line in the Lord's prayer...

Which line is Digit thinking of? Fill in the missing vowels (a e i o u) to find out.

```
F-rg-v-  -s  th-   wr-ngs
w-  h-v-  d-n-,  -s  w-
f-rg-v-  th-  wr-ngs  th-t
    -th-rs  h-v-  d-n-
         t-   -s.
```

Matthew 6:12

Quartz suddenly had a thought.

Simeon said that Jesus was a light to the Gentiles—who are they?

Well, that's a general name for everybody who isn't Jewish. Like the Samaritans.

Who are the Samaritans?

I remember hearing a story at school that Jesus told about the Good Samaritan.

That's right! The Samaritans live in Northern Israel and in the past often worshipped idols. That was one of the reasons that the Jewish people would have nothing to do with them.

But Jesus did!

Yes! Jesus always showed concern for those who were hated and he often travelled through Samaria and stayed with the Samaritans.

Jesus was like my torch—shining his light into dark places.

And telling people the secret about how much God loves them—no matter who they are.

Yes, but Jesus' story about the Good Samaritan shows us the other part of that secret, too.

Luke 10:27

Love the Lord your God with all your heart, with all your soul, with all your strength, and with all your mind; and love your neighbour as you love yourself.

Dear Lord, help me to love other people as much as I love myself, even when this means...

61

Look out for more Bible Adventures with the
LIVEWIRES

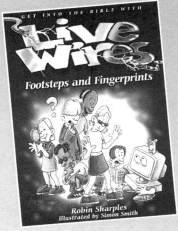

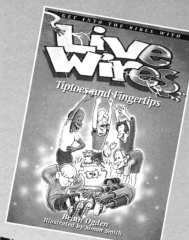

Footsteps and Fingerprints

Families and Feelings

Tiptoes and Fingertips

Friends and Followers

Available from your local Christian bookshop or, in case of difficulty, direct from BRF, Peter's Way, Sandy Lane West, Oxford OX4 5HG. If you want to order by credit card why not telephone your order direct to BRF?

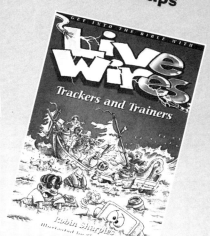

Trackers and Trainers

Bible Reading Fellowship is a Registered Charity